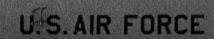

U.S. AIR FORCE

6014

FORCE

0453

To Al and Roberta
Thank you for staying at the
State Street Inn.
Mike and Yvonne Hall
Dover, De.

The Colors of Kent

World-class Winston Cup stock car racing at Dover Downs International Speedway revs up each June and September.

Kevin Fleming

text by Nancy E. Lynch • edited by Lori Epstein

ISBN 0-9662423-3-5
copyright ©MCMXCIX by Kevin Fleming

In Delaware's agrarian heartland, Kent County's small-town charm blends seamlessly with government and industry. Festivals, fairs and parades stitch a human face on the First State's middle county where farmers, legislators, professionals, artisans and watermen weave a colorful fabric from everyday endeavor.

"We say Jeremy's got that Opie look. And he can pick a pretty good quart of berries," Jennifer Hobbs says of her youngest son's finesse in the family's one-acre strawberry field near Viola (preceding pages). The short-season fruit ripens by Memorial Day and attracts hundreds to the Hobbs' U-pick operation. "They'll pick up to dusk or until the field gets picked out. It's something we've done on the side for about six years. We enjoy seeing the same people every year. They like their strawberries."

Digging in her family's Felton area potato farm, Jennifer Black (right) gets in touch with roots sown by her grandfather, Francis Bergold, a Kent County transplant from Long Island 50 years ago. "The land was reasonable and it's good here to raise crops," says the patriarch of Byfield Farms, first established on Delaware patriot Caesar Rodney's lands near Kitts Hummock. Bergold markets 250 acres of all-purpose potatoes from Maine to Florida and also grows wheat, barley and field corn. "I help out whenever I'm home," says Black, a college sophomore. "I grew up with potatoes and love to live on a farm. You have open space and it's so peaceful."

"It's an eye-catcher, not real little, not real big, but it's what people like best," incurable collector Bill Paskey says of the rare 1940s Model S Case tractor wedged in his Felton farm museum (left) with thousands of antique toys, tools, trucks and other tractors. "There's so much stuff, it's just overwhelming. It's a private hobby just for show, never for sale. I keep bringing more stuff home from flea markets. People give me a lot too."

A fifth-generation grain farmer and tavern owner, Paskey relaxes with daughter Taylor Lynn (preceding pages) in the backyard he's named Deer Park, a 3-acre hamlet of vintage buildings, railroad siding and rolling stock. "The theme's like a time machine. Imagine yourself in an old farmhouse or one-room schoolhouse or country store. We even have an old captain's shack from Bowers Beach. The boxcar, caboose and old locomotive are filled too, mostly with train collectibles and pictures." Paskey welcomes the community to Deer Park for church picnics and school field trips. "I collect whenever I can get away," he says. "I've always been able to save up for my pastime. I'm never done collecting."

Rolling into another season, Dicky Moor (right) readies Leipsic crab boats for the catch in Delaware Bay and beyond. "Usually we're out by the first of May," he says. "All depends on the water temperature and if there's going to be any crabs. You get a real cold winter, a lot of ice, and that kills a lot of crabs." Moor baits 200 pots with bunkers or menhaden and sets them four miles out in the bay. He checks them daily, shoving off at 5 a.m. "There's a lot of miserable days but you'll put up with it if you're catching something," says Moor. He's done crabbing in October. "It's according to how the crabs are running and what the price is. Your crab buyer will let you know. He just keeps dropping the price." A former eeler, Moor has few complaints. "I got into full-time crabbing about 14 years ago. I've had one bad year, pretty good years and really good years."

Divided by the Murderkill River, Bowers Beach and South Bowers (preceding pages) harbor much of Kent County's crab industry.

"You want a good count in your basket," veteran waterman Jim Dare of Magnolia explains as he readies a collar for a catch of crabs (right). "You take the top half of a basket, turn it upside down and put it over the basket you're filling to make it overflow. You want a nice count before you put the lid on." Dare works aboard a Chesapeake crab boat built in the 1970s near Crisfield, Maryland. "She's long and narrow so she can push through the water easily and has a fairly flat bottom so she can get into shallow water without rubbing too bad." During the season, he sets out 200 pots, the maximum allowed by Delaware law. "The spring run is mainly sooks or females. Next will be peelers – crabs getting ready to shed – then the summer jimmy run, the blue-claw males. This area's always been real high-producing for crabs," says Dare, a Vietnam veteran whose great-great-grandfather built Saxton United Methodist Church in Bowers Beach. "From Big Stone Beach to Kitts Hummock is a cove with the Balkenbrig Ditch, the Murderkill and St. Jones rivers running to the Delaware Bay. Crabs tend to go to brackish water. A lot of bait hangs out there and peelers go there to shed."

At dawn, a crabber (following pages) churns east from Bowers Beach to check his pots. "You want to be on the water before the sun comes up and at your first pot at daylight," says Dare, who also holds commercial licenses to fish, eel and conch. "It's a grind. Most people won't do this work. I have brothers who won't go near it but I love it. You don't have to put up with an office or paperwork and every day there's something new and different to adapt to to get the job done. It's a feeling of freedom."

"I'm told a new broom sweeps clean," says Wesley College president Scott D. Miller (left). "I've made a lot of changes and the school has grown by 700 students in the two years I've been here." Founded in 1873, the private, United Methodist Church-affiliated college in downtown Dover now enrolls 1,700 students. Nationally ranked football and basketball teams supplement the liberal arts curriculum. "Dover's a wonderful place to live. We were attracted because of the beauty of the community and the college and the quality of life here." Miller, past president of Tennessee's Lincoln Memorial University, and his family are the first occupants of the Annie Jump Cannon house since its 1997 donation to the college. The 6,000-square-foot president's residence in Dover's historic district is a block from campus. Cannon, a shipbuilder's daughter, grew up in the house. An internationally acclaimed astronomer who died in 1941, she analyzed 286,000 stars and shines as one of Wesley College's best-known alumni.

"It's pretty much 'This Old House' except without Norm and his crew," Smyrna resident Scott Clark says of his mid-1800s Federal fixer-upper on Commerce Street (following pages). He and his wife, Sandra, bought the house in 1996. "We were actually looking at the house across the street then turned around and saw a 'For Sale' sign in front of this one. We cleaned the dirt off the window and saw 10-foot ceilings, 12-inch plaster crown molding, two slate fireplaces and a humongous living room. We fell in love with it." Framed by raised panel plantation shutters, the lumberyard manager pulls maintenance on windows too large to be original. "I'll be restoring this house for the next 20 years. You'll have to take the spackle knife out of my hand when I die. But even if I finish just a small piece of it, I've restored something that deserves to be restored and brought it back to its glory."

Pedal power cycles Dover police officers Gerald Perry and Chris White (preceding pages) closer to the city's 33,000 residents. "The bottom line," Dover Police chief Keith I. Faulkner says, "is bicycles put us in touch with the community and the community with us." Of the 81 law enforcement officers the Smyrna native commands, five are assigned to the Dover Police Department's bike patrol. A federal grant bought the first bicycles in 1990. "The officers on this team are specialized and enjoy biking, riding both day and night. Having a bicycle patrol gives folks a chance to meet the officers. When they're in a police car, there's a barrier." Faulkner commends an "absolutely wonderful" civilian support staff for assisting police coverage of the state capital's 27 square miles. "Dover's growing," he says. "We have great officers and very supportive residents. I look at the city as a very safe, very good community."

"It's the only tire swing in the neighborhood," says Cathy Cole (right), catching a ride with friend Kristi Ayala as her twin, Cassi, looks on. The popular pendulum hangs from a black oak tree in the sisters' Smryna front yard and receives year-round workouts. "My mom's boyfriend, Kenny, made it about two years ago and we always swing on it. It's fun to watch people swing too," says Cassi. "You can push off the ground with your feet but if somebody works the rope, you can go 17 feet up in the air," Cathy adds. "That's the best part, getting really high up. It's a really weird feeling. It pulls on your stomach and the wind's in your face."

Squatters rights take a front seat near Marydel for Shari Wilbur, Joel Marousek and their sons, Critter, Little Hippie and Squirt (left). "Joel works as a custodian and brings toilets home all the time. We don't advertise but people drive by and see them," Shari says. "It took a little while for the first ones to sell but they've finally started going. They're only $20 and people buy them for remodeling and for personal use. We use the extra income for odds and ends."

"Nobody wants to do what I do 'cause it's too much trouble," says basketmaker Floyd Hrupsa (following pages) of Felton. "Takes me three to four hours on each basket, time I saw from the tree 'till I finish." Hrupsa, whose grandfather, Thomas Minner, operated a basket mill at Masten's Corner, fashions three sizes of baskets from red cedar or walnut using a form from Minner's mill. "See the Xs? That means they're handmade. Can't do that on a machine." Hrupsa demonstrates his dying art at Delaware, Maryland and Pennsylvania antique shows where his large baskets retail for $25. A retired state employee, Hrupsa stables a 1952 Dodge truck in a neighbor's lean-to. "Used it to haul grain when I was farming on the side. Don't want to get rid of it 'cause it's antique and still in good shape. Odometer's been 'round once so it's really got 152,000 miles."

Frank Hrupsa (above) stands behind his broomstraw. "They'll last according to how heavy you use 'em, normally several years," he says. It's a hobby, not a living," says Hrupsa, 83, who sells large, decorative and whiskbrooms at special events like Old Dover Days. Each large broom consumes a pound and a half of the broomstraw he grows near Harrington and 45 minutes of his time. "A couple hundred a year is 'bout all I can produce and I very near sell them all. People say I make brooms the old-fashioned way. That makes me feel good."

Spinner Cyndi Angermeier (right) winds down next to Voshell's Mill near Rising Sun. "My great-grandfather, grandfather and father operated it as a grist mill, then a seed mill," she says of the 19th century mill she converted to her unique residence in the mid-1980s. The Caesar Rodney School District psychologist pastures two sheep there and demonstrates her spinning hobby at the Delaware Agricultural Museum and Village, Old Dover Days and in the classroom. "When I'm spinning, I'm sharing history. In Colonial times, families paid taxes in part with wool. It's something our ancestors had to do." At home, Angermeier finds spinning therapeutic. "It's extremely relaxing, almost mesmerizing."

"I'm a traditional tinsmith but I've added a contemporary flair for the millennium," Richard L. Haddick (left) of Wyoming says of the electrified lanterns he fashions from lithographed cans. "Everything I make is traditional and built in the time period 1780 to 1865 with traditional tools." Available in eight tin patterns, Haddick's lanterns require four to six hours of labor and retail for $100 to $175. He works seven days a week in his workshop on Wyoming Mill Pond. "I don't have a sign or a phone and the only things electric in my shop are my soldering iron, stereo and lights. I come to work at 7 p.m., read the newspaper and listen to music. I start at 10 and work until 5 a.m. That's when I seem to be at my most creative." Haddick teaches his trade at the Fletcher Farm School for Arts and Crafts in Ludlow, Vermont and at the Carroll County Farm Museum in Westminster, Maryland. "People call me the Tinman. Everybody asks what's my favorite piece. I tell them the piece I'm working on now. I love my job."

Dover folk artist Nina Spencer (following pages) is known for her tile and canvas paintings in primary colors. "All my art tells stories. I do a lot of spiritual and religious themes like baptisms in water and old country churches," says the self-taught Baptist preacher's daughter from Louisiana. "I also do some Old South, like cotton picking. My work is very simple and honest." State commissions include the Underground Railroad on tiles. "If you want tiles, I'm the girl. Angels guide my hand and my paint just flows." An artist since she was 12, Spencer credits her father for inspiring her career. "I talked too much so my daddy got me a little paint set, some overalls and set up an easel and that's how it's been ever since."

Framed by Delaware illustrator Frank Schoonover's works, curator Roxanne Stanulis (preceding pages at left) and director Karol Schmiegel usher impressionist Robert Reid's "A Summer Girl" to another gallery at the Sewell C. Biggs Museum of American Art in Dover. More than 500 objects are displayed on two floors above the Delaware State Visitor Center on Duke of York Street. Paintings, furniture and silver fill 14 galleries of the museum which opened in 1993. "The museum is unique in that it is based on the collection of one man, Sewell C. Biggs," says Stanulis. "The focus is regional with a very good representation of objects by Delaware artists." The Schoonover Gallery, she adds, is the only gallery in the Dover museum wholly devoted to one artist.

Assistant Bruce Decker (right) creates his own still life with 18th century objects in the museum's first gallery. The circa 1750 tall clock on the right contains works by George Crow, one of Wilmington's earliest clockmakers. Duncan Beard of Appoquinimink made the movement for the 1770s tall clock. Crafted in Delaware before 1765, the Queen Anne chairs descended through the Loockerman family of Dover. New Castle-born Anna Dorothea Finney chose blue for her circa 1760 portrait by John Hesselius.

Smyrna sculptor Richard H. Bailey (following pages) loses his abstract and realistic marbles to scores of satisfied customers who pay premium prices for a chip off his blocks. "People like marble. I have more than 100 varieties," he says. "I also work in granite, onyx, jade, jasper and semiprecious stones but primarily in marble." Bailey exhibits his popular stone sculptures at numerous East Coast galleries, including New York City's Museum of Natural History. Shadowed by 3-ton marble columns from a Philadelphia library, he sands an original cross of white marble. The native Kent Countian prefers working outdoors, housing diamond and silicon carbide saws and more than 120 tools in a converted pony barn on his mother's farm.

Bargain-hunter Paul Franklin (right) of the Blackbird area strums a potential buy at Spence's Bazaar and Auction in Dover. "Some come just for the auction, some come just for the flea market, some come just for the farmer's market. And some come for all three," says Gregory Spence, third-generation owner with his sisters, Ann Scott and Phyllis Spence. Scott's husband, Jack, is manager. Open Tuesdays and Fridays year-round, the bazaar has been a Dover tradition since 1933 when Gregory's grandfather, Harry Spence, first auctioned livestock at his farm off South New Street. Both the auction and Harry's big red barn, the reconstructed tomato cannery he moved from Fleming's Landing, are hallmarks. "We're known for bargains," Spence says. Hundreds pack the property weekly and devotees travel from as far as Rhode Island. The farmer's market, featuring Amish meats, baked goods and cooked food, was added in 1976. Now the family's fourth generation is involved in the business. "Three of us have been running it for 19 years. Far as I can see, it's there for our kids when we're gone."

"You couldn't pay me to work that hard," volunteer farrier Terry Dunham (right) says inside the circa 1850 Johnson & Son Blacksmith shop at the Delaware Agricultural Museum and Village in Dover. As a demonstrator for the nonprofit museum, Dunham uses the shop's coal forge, hand-cranked blower and antique tools to make nails, hooks, trivets and tongs for a year-round audience. "I enjoy explaining what life was like in the 1800s," says the Kenton resident, a quality control laboratory technician for a New Castle County plastics firm. "Working with hot iron is my artistic outlet. It puts me in touch with history."

Relics from another trade (above) line shelves at the nearby Gourley Barbershop where men gathered for a haircut, a shave and two-bit talk. Centerpiece of the private educational organization is the re-created 19th century village of Loockerman Landing. The Dover museum's mission is the preservation and interpretation of Delaware and Delmarva's agricultural heritage. The museum also preserves the Jehu F. Camper Folk Art Collection, a nationally recognized display of wood carvings by the late Harrington resident.

Greatest show on First State turf, the Delaware State Fair amuses, thrills, entertains and educates crowds topping 200,000 during its 10-day run each July. Incorporated in 1919 as the non-profit Kent & Sussex County Fair, the agrarian-based event tempts all ages to the 90-acre fairgrounds in Harrington. Animal husbandry, farm equipment and crop exhibits are constants, but grandstand entertainment is a rising star with recent sell-out shows by Reba McEntire, Alabama, and Boyz II Men.

"The fair represents a homecoming to many people," says general manager Dennis Hazzard. "It's such a family event. Many return because they like the atmosphere and they like taking in the whole experience as a family. People still have an interest in letting their kids know where milk comes from."

Kelsey Grace of Smyrna (left) shows off Brady's Lady at the Delaware State Fair's Pretty Animal Contest. Placing second was, well, second place. "I think we should have won," Kelsey says after losing to a mule. "But I was having fun. I look forward to the fair."

"It's just all fun," agrees Eric Hitch of Houston (above), mugging with Mickey, his 5-month-old market lamb. Prepping Mickey for the show ring took time. "We bathed him quite a bit with dish detergent, toweled him off and let him drip dry in the sun," explains Eric, a Hummingbirds 4-H Club member seven of his 12 years. "Then we brushed him with a scrub brush to make him fluffy. He was pretty good in the ring, just a little nervous. I was a lot nervous."

Young farmers man a cow wash (following pages) at the fair where bovines milk a lot of attention. Dairy farming is a $25 million slice of Delaware's agricultural pie with about 95 dairy farms producing nearly 14 million gallons of milk annually. After primping, these young Holsteins hoof to the show ring to compete by breed and age for cash and ribbons. "Cows are one of the most viewed exhibits at the fair," says Bill Vanderwende, one of 80 fair directors and dairy division superintendent. "Kids and adults love to see animals. Other state fairs are more commercial. We have tried to maintain ours as an agricultural fair."

"We're outdoorsy people and we love horses, nature and Sunday strolls on The Neck," says Trina Mitchell, (pages 52 and 53) astride her quarterhorse Mint. Framed by a tunnel of oak, gum and swamp maples near Leipsic, she intersects husband Sammy's path on Blaze. Roots run deep for the native Kent Countians. "I've lived here all my life. It's a very beautiful spot with woods and fields and marshes. For me, the freedom of being on a horse in this area is relaxing. The horse takes over and you just go."

Trainer John E. Veazey of Laurel warms up his standardbred Niacrombie (preceding pages) on Harrington Raceway's half-mile stone dust track. "Our most important race," general manager Karen Craft says, "is the $40,000 Governor's Cup during the Delaware State Fair. It's a very nice purse." The track, established on the fairgrounds in 1946 as the Kent and Sussex Raceway, clocks 90 days of spring and fall racing. "Our purses average in excess of $100,000 a night. That's very favorable to the horsemen and gives them a chance to upgrade their stock and enhance harness racing," says the Greenwood native. "The best part of my day is the first race of the night. There's just something about the thundering of hooves and manes blowing in the wind."

Delaware's horseracing industry trotted past extinction in 1995 when the General Assembly passed the Horse Racing Preservation Act legalizing slot machines at Harrington Raceway, Dover Downs in Dover and Delaware Park in Stanton. With slots revenues tallying $300 million in 1997, the tracks galloped to victory and now rein in more visitors than the state's fabled beaches. And with a 91.5 percent return on every dollar wagered, slots players smile too.

"The best part is winning, of course, and most all the time I come away a winner," Pat Prowell (left) says between bets at Dover Downs Slots. The Mt. Wolf, Pennsylvania resident summers in Woodland Beach and spends six hours two or three times a week at the Las Vegas-style casino. "I used to go to Atlantic City, but I'm committed to Dover Downs because everybody's nice and it's not crowded." Next to her, Marylanders Maggie and Kenny Welch test their quarter power at one of Dover Downs' 1,000 video lottery terminals.

Mustard on the side, trainer Karen Moore puts harness racer Displain (following pages) through different paces near Smyrna. "A cross country pleasure ride freshens him up so he doesn't get bored going around the track." Still racing, the 10-year-old standardbred stallion is also a lucrative Delaware Stakes Program sire. "We horsemen have all this money because of the slots which we petitioned. We were a long time getting them."

In the pink, peach trees at Fifer Orchards west of Wyoming spring into production, yielding 72,000 baskets of 25 varieties of peaches during the 10-week season starting in late June. "It's really a wonderful heritage we have. There's something special about being linked to growing things," says Mary Fennemore, third generation owner with her brother, Carlton Fifer (left). His oldest sons, David and Bobby, also work in the business established in 1919 by patriarch Charles Frederick Fifer Sr., a farmer from Virginia's Shenandoah Valley. Apples, sweet corn, peaches and asparagus headline the harvest from the family's 2,500-acre spread. Strawberries, cantaloupes, tomatoes, plums, potatoes, nectarines, broccoli, pears and pumpkins are also available in season. "People enjoy coming to a farm setting even if they can go to a grocery store and buy just about anything," Fennemore says. "But you can't beat the freshness here." Peaches vaulted Kent County to world prominence in 1869 with more than a million trees in production. Although a disease called "the Yellows" later ended Delaware's reign as the Peach State, the General Assembly in 1895 adopted the peach blossom as the state flower. "We started a customer appreciation day back in the early 1980s and served peach ice cream cones," says Carlton. "In 1990, the town of Wyoming started the Peach Festival. We combined the two events and the festival's grown every year." Now Fifer Orchards scoops 10,000 free cones each August using more than 500 gallons of peach ice cream. "People around here like ice cream. I sure had my share that day."

Irish eyes smiling, Marissa Grinstead and Danielle Patterson (right) of Daisy Troop 1092 prepare to step off in the St. Patrick's Day Parade in Dover. "Everybody's Irish on St. Patrick's Day," says Lorraine Goodman, director of Main Street Dover, sponsor of the 90-minute parade that lines Loockerman Street with a crowd of 7,000. "Not more than 20 of us, including Irish wolfhounds, marched the first year, 1994," recalls Mary Fitzpatrick, past president of the 80-member Irish Society of Delmarva. "Now, your adrenaline's going and there's a lot of camaraderie," adds the Dublin native who always dresses as a leprechaun and dances a jig. "The crowd really gets into it with clapping and singing."

Danielle Herrmann and Ashley Krueger (preceding pages) of Girl Scout Troop 421 doff hats before marching in the 87-unit parade while Robert Swarthout and his granddaughter, Bridgett Durham, (following pages) share a special moment on the sidelines. "Far as I know, I'm a Swede," says Swarthout. "But I thought the parade was wonderful. Bridgett got a big kick out of the clowns, puppies and fire trucks and so did I."

"Our claim to fame is maypole dancing on May Day. It's the single thing that makes us different," says Mary Skelton, chairman of Old Dover Days (preceding pages), a three-day festival celebrating Dover's Colonial heritage. "I never have to worry about attendance for the maypole dance because we have several area elementary schools participating and all the children's parents, grandparents, brothers and sisters show up." Complemented by Colonial crafts demonstrations, a juried Arts Festival and a parade, the event, inaugurated by Friends of Old Dover in 1933, draws 10,000 to The Green, Legislative Mall and other venues. "We're the city's largest and oldest festival and probably one of the oldest in the nation," Skelton says. "We've even been on 'Jeopardy.'"

Diane Bacher-Mikaelian (left) of Dover hosts Victorian tea parties for local young ladies at Camden's historic Rose Tower Bed and Breakfast. "I try to instill in them a sense of history and etiquette and have fun doing it," she says. Her two-hour parties include dressing in Victorian finery, fashioning ribboned headpieces, playing 19th century games and sipping tea from fine china. "I do love history and get a real special feeling when I dress up. I moved to Delaware from Florida because I wanted a change of pace. Something smaller, friendly and with a hometown feeling. That's why Dover's such a wonderful place to live. And it's filled with history."

Called the "Cradle of Methodism," Barratt's Chapel (preceding pages) near Frederica begat the Methodist Episcopal Church in America. An inlaid brass star on the floor marks the meeting of Bishop Thomas Coke and clergyman Francis Asbury who formulated plans on November 14, 1784 for a church separate from the Anglicans' Protestant Episcopal Church. Coke for the first time administered sacraments in an American Methodist service. Land for the chapel in South Murderkill Hundred was conveyed in 1780 by Phillip Barratt, a converted Methodist farmer and Kent County sheriff. Built the same year, the nearly square Georgian structure stands as the nation's oldest house of worship constructed for and by a Methodist Society.

"Our family's not gotten 50 miles in 300 years," quips Armstrong Barratt Cullen III (right) of Rehoboth Beach inside Barratt's Chapel with his father, Armstrong Barratt Cullen Jr. of Dover, and son, Armstrong Barratt Cullen IV, 14, direct descendents of Phillip Barratt. Phillip's son, John Barratt, whose portrait hangs over the eldest Cullen's living room fireplace, was Delaware's secretary of state in 1810. His daughter was Mary Barratt Cullen. "It was kinda cool, how the building looked and the worn-down stones in the cemetery," the youngest Cullen says of his first visit to Barratt's Chapel. "I don't know many fourths. I have my full name on my State of Delaware boater's license but that's the only thing. If I have a son, I'd consider passing my name on. It's been passed on for hundreds of years. That's kinda cool."

"When all the kids come here to worship, I may have five Aaron's age or younger so sometimes I have to get loud," Pastor Bruce Tribbitt says of his more vocal charges at Manship Chapel west of Felton. Small wonder Aaron Brown, 2, of Harrington (left) saves his amens and favorite bean-bag dog for family worship at the 1855 chapel with original pews that seat 120 "if everybody's friendly. This used to be Manship United Methodist Church but it closed about 1995 and we're an independent, King James Bible-believing church," says Tribbitt. "We're very conservative, along the lines of Fundamentalists, but wanted to keep the name because Andrew Manship preached here and at Barratt's Chapel." Preaching here is important to Tribbitt too, "but I also enjoy the fellowship. We go away on retreats together. We're like one big family."

On promised land, members of the Jireh Christian Center (following pages) celebrate their first worship service. Eight days of rejoicing reverberated over the 42-acre site west of Dover, acquired in 1985 soon after the center was established. "We had 60 members, young families, and $50 in our church checking account then, but knew we wanted land to build on," says Pastor Miriam Mast. "People got excited about our vision and handed us $1,000 checks. We came up with a $40,000 down payment – I consider that a huge miracle – and we paid off the rest of the land in 1991." With a building fund of nearly $90,000, members plan to worship in a new center by year's end. "We've been meeting in the old theater at the Blue Hen Mall. People don't want to go back," Mast says of the 200-member flock she ministers with ordained husband Dale. "Jireh is a Hebrew word that means 'the Lord who sees and provides.' We know people aren't happy-clappy. One of our goals is to see they get healing so they can become free to lead fruitful, productive lives."

Boyhood home of 18th century Delaware patriot John Dickinson, Poplar Hall on Jones Neck southeast of Dover (right) survives as a National Historic Landmark and state museum. A Tory looting of the Georgian mansion in 1781 prompted Dickinson, one of Kent County's largest landowners, to accept the Delaware presidency after Caesar Rodney's term expired to bolster Delaware's militia during the Revolutionary period. Also president of Pennsylvania, he was among the last state presidents. Article 3 of the U.S. Constitution, ratified in 1792, changed the title to governor. Throughout his public life, Dickinson also maintained homes in Wilmington and Philadelphia. In 1804, a spark from the parlor chimney ignited Poplar Hall's cedar shake roof, burning the 1740 dwelling's wooden infrastructure, leaving only the brick walls. An easterly wind contained the fire to the house's oldest section. Dickinson rebuilt the home two years later, redesigning the roofline as it appears today. Once more than 3,000 acres along the St. Jones River, Dickinson's plantation of cherry, plum, peach and apple orchards also produced wheat, corn and flax. Slaves and tenants farmed the land, inhabiting dirt floor dwellings (preceding pages) with enclosed plots for their root vegetables and herbs. Other outbuildings on the restored site that opened in 1956 include a granary, feed barn, stable, smokehouse and corncrib. "We're privileged having a lot of information on John Dickinson's plantation," says site supervisor Edward McWilliams. "That makes the museum, which is open year-round, very unique. We know what happened here."

Three-quarter ton bales of straw, remains of grain crop harvests, weather the elements near Dover (following pages). A valuable commodity for the multi-million dollar mushroom industry to the north, bales like these are trucked out of Kent County throughout the winter months. Southeastern Pennsylvania mushroom producers grind and mix the straw with manure for compost.

"We have national recognition as an important area for migrating birds," says Bombay Hook National Wildlife Refuge wildlife biologist Frank Smith. "It's a famous place for people who know a lot about waterfowl and shorebirds." Snow geese (preceding pages) arrive in early October from Arctic Circle and northern Canada nesting grounds and their population peaks at 198,000 a month later. "They consume a lot of food while they're here and compete with Canada geese for corn and winter wheat, but they do some good things, like open areas of dense vegetation to allow other species to come in and feed."

Other refuge residents include the more solitary great blue heron (right). "We have maybe 100 and you'll see them in the water feeding on frogs, fish and small snakes," Smith says. "They're common throughout the state. Some will spend the entire winter here. If things freeze up, they'll move south." Bombay Hook offers safe haven to more than 100,000 migrating and wintering waterfowl (following pages). Established in northeastern Kent County in 1937, Bombay Hook is one of more than 500 refuges administered by the U.S. Fish and Wildlife Service. Tidal salt marsh, a valuable wildlife habitat, comprises three-quarters of the refuge's nearly 16,000 acres, plaited by rivers, creeks, branches, ditches and guts. Refuge management programs, designed to develop and protect desirable migratory waterfowl habitat, include raising crops on 1,100 acres for supple-mental food. A visitor center, 12-mile auto tour route, observation towers and nature trails are open to the public year-round.

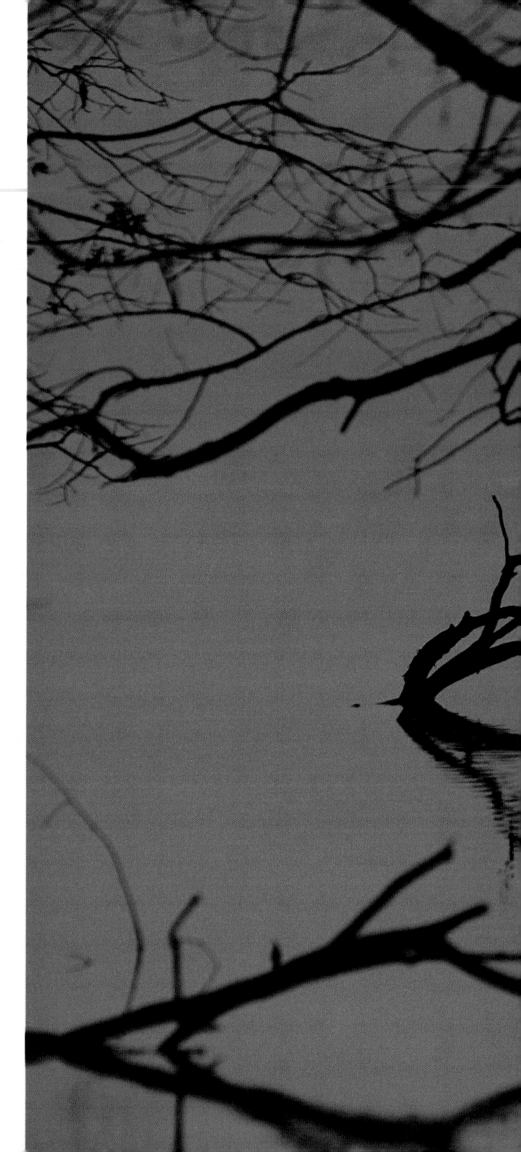

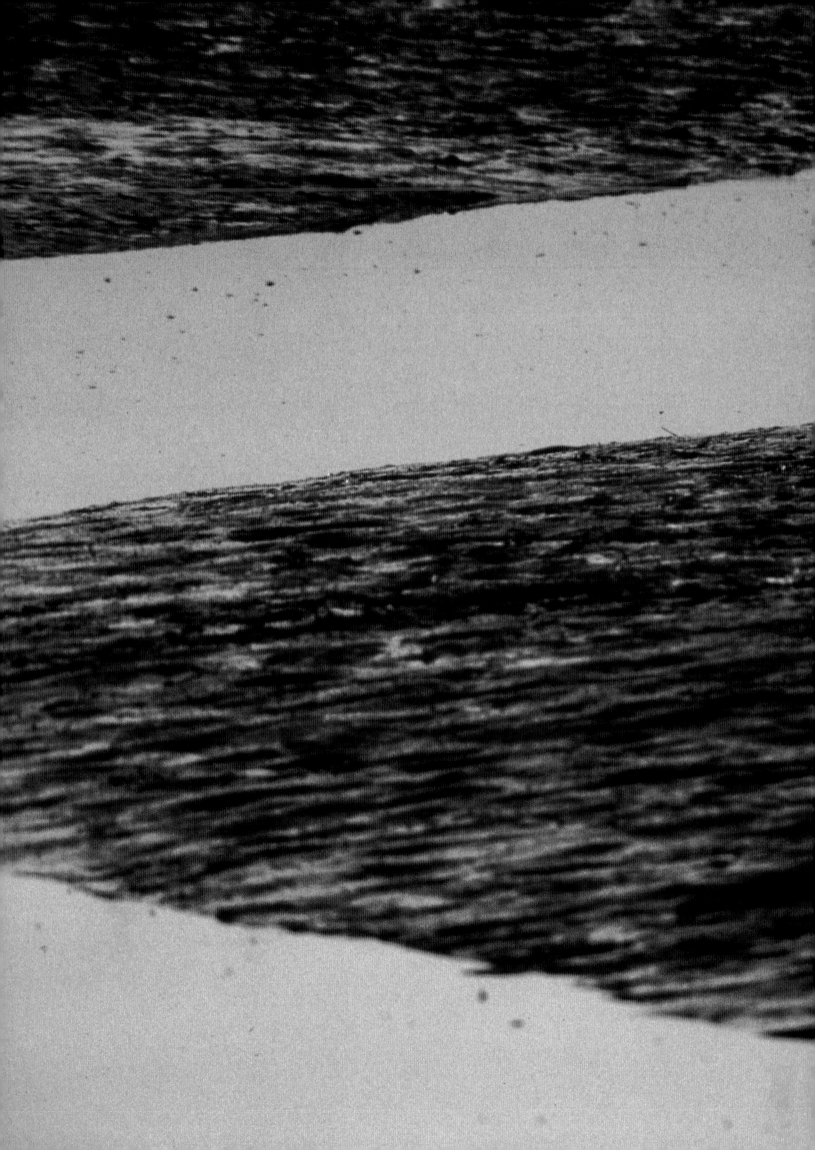

Meandering toward Delaware Bay, nearby Taylor's Gut (preceding pages) laces Woodland Beach Wildlife Area, supporting tidal flats, woods with habitat for the soapwort gentian, a rare, fall-blooming wildflower, and a pageant of wildlife. Dudley C. Lunt recorded the unspoiled area's majesty in his 1968 narrative, **_Taylor's Gut_**. Trumpeting fall, tree-lined fields near Bombay Hook (left) define their golden boundaries.

Corn shocks stud a farm west of Dover (preceding pages) where horsepower is four-footed and Old Order Amish ways have prevailed since Jacob K. Miller moved to Kent County from California on February 8, 1915 and bought the first Amish farm 10 days later. Still a significant agricultural community, Amish families own at least 100 farms, down from about 300 farms 10 years ago, and cultivate about four thousand acres.

Encroaching development and escalating land prices force increasing numbers to flee the area, leaving Amish boys near Pearson's Corner (right) facing an uncertain future.

"Got over an acre here and it ain't little, not when you go to cuttin' grass," Lester Allen (left) of Clayton fusses as he whacks weeds at his Duck Creek Road home. "I'm cuttin' 'round Susie's pen. She's fat, 75 pounds, for a bassett hound but she's nine years old." Allen, who retired in 1982 after nearly 33 years with General Motors in Newport, and wife Sara also collect wooden cutouts crafted by Kent County Amish. "She bought the horse and buggy 'bout four or five years ago 'cause she loved it. She bought a man too. He's out to the corner of the house. She's got five or six deer out front and wheelbarrows. This is the only place we know. It's home and when it's home, you love it."

Brotherly love smiles in Clayton where Marvin and Michael Poore pause outside Sylvia's Beauty Parlor on Main Street. "All in all, Clayton's not a bad place to raise kids. There's not a lot of trouble here," says neighbor Dawn Burke, mother of three and a resident all but two of her 25 years. "We're 20 to 25 minutes from Dover and 30 to 45 minutes from anything important in New Castle County." Southern States, Clement's Supply Company and the Corner Store are principal businesses in the town of about 1,300 bisected by Norfolk Southern railroad. "Biggest thing that's happened here is the 100th anniversary of the Clayton Volunteer Fire Company. They had a town-wide cookout in the parking lot of Metal Masters." The town holds a tree-lighting festival at Christmas and partners with Smyrna for Fourth of July celebrations. "It's quiet here," Burke says. "Everybody knows their neighbors. Clayton's one of those you-do-for-me and I'll-do-for-you places."

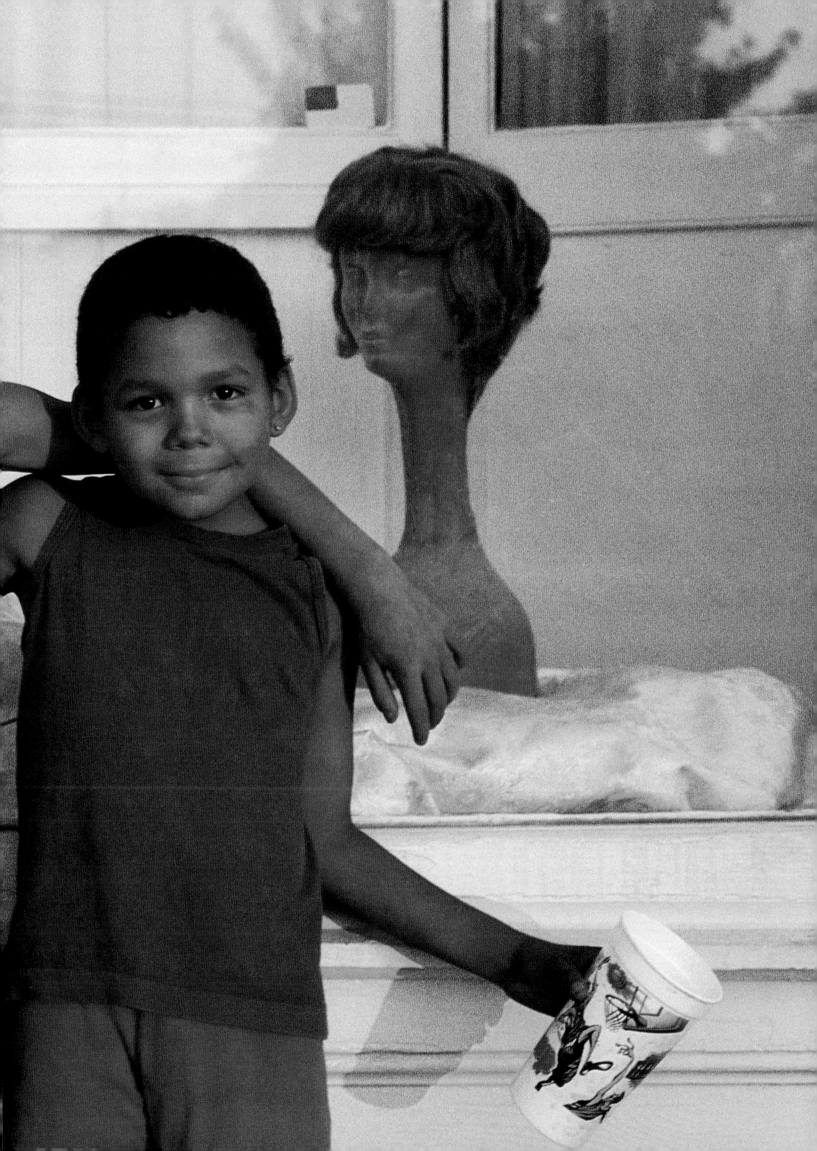

Golden harvest, soybeans reap healthy dividends for Delaware farmers (preceding pages) growing the state's largest cash crop on more than 220,000 acres. The legume's average annual yield of seven million bushels is processed into poultry and livestock feed and diverse soy protein products. "Soybeans are Delaware's top crop because historically they bring about twice as much per bushel as corn," says Felton farmer Bob Garey who cultivates 1,300 acres. "They don't have the yield production of other crops but seed costs less and they take less fertilizer. Soybeans are used in ink, glue, lubricants, fuel and paint, but their food value is the best part."

Soil sweetener, dry limestone powders a field near Woodland Beach (right) soon after sunrise. "The only time we don't spread is when crops are in the field," says Martin Limestone manager Sim Chisenhall. Martin Limestone operates a 10,000-ton capacity warehouse at the edge of a woods near Viola and spreads up to five times that amount every year from Dover south to Virginia's Eastern Shore. "We're probably the number one company for dry limestone from the Chesapeake Bay to New York," Chisenhall says. "The more farmers doublecrop, the more they need lime to neutralize the soil. It's like putting a teaspoon of sugar in a cup of coffee."

Pushing the envelope, ILC Dover workers inspect the laminated polyester skin of a 125-foot-long airship manufactured at the Frederica facility (following pages). "We're pinholing for defects with a 500-watt light," says project engineer Tim Miller. "Crews inside and out look for pinholes, like stars in the sky. Every square inch of the balloon gets a light inspection." With a helium volume of 68,000 cubic feet, this airship is ILC's smallest, just half the length of its largest. "Blockbuster, Budweiser, Sanyo, MetLife – you see them at sporting events. They're ours," Miller says. "Airships are only about 10 percent of ILC's business. We're best known for our space suits." "But airships are very unique," adds production manager Stella Rexrode. "And interest is growing."

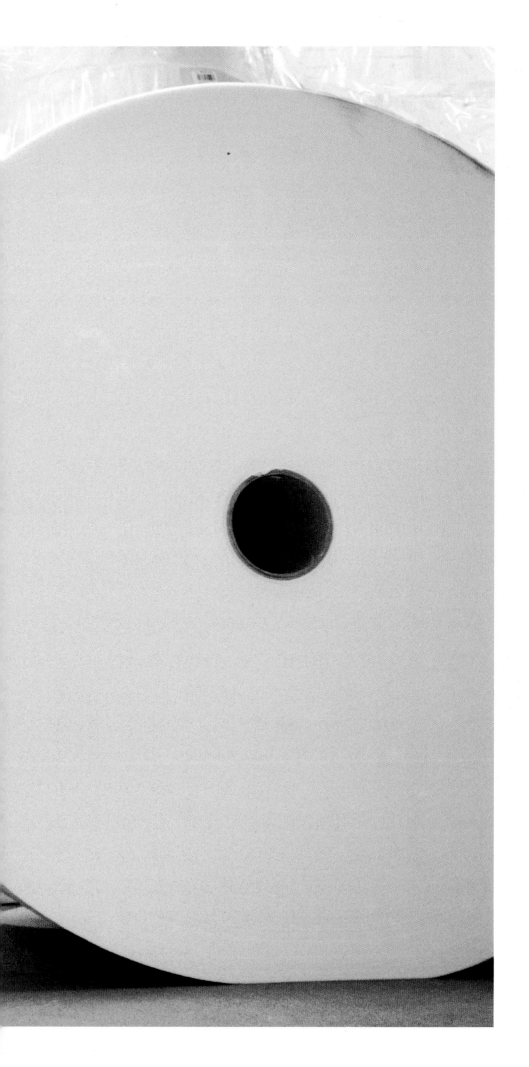

At the Procter & Gamble Dover Wipes Company, production technician Bob Baines (left) is dwarfed by a roll of the material used in the manufacture of Pampers Baby Fresh Wipes. "One of these rolls affords the opportunity for many, many thousands of diaper changes since our product is used by moms and dads to care for their babies' skin," says company spokeswoman Justine Maggio. "We have a three-part operation here. We make, we pack and we ship." More than 300 employees support the operation at the West North Street site. "We were part of Scott Paper Company from 1972 to 1995 when we were sold to Kimberly-Clark. In 1996, Procter & Gamble aquired the Dover Wipes Company," Maggio says. "It's an excellent place to work with a great group of people and outstanding benefits. But it would have to be for me to drive 140 miles every day to work here."

"We refer to it as the Royal Charter Document. It is the actual document whereby King Charles II in 1682 transferred to his brother James, Duke of York, most of what is today the state of Delaware," says Delaware Public Archives spokesman Russ McCabe (left). "It is certainly one of our two most valuable documents, along with the state's 1787 U.S. Constitution ratification document. And it's in beautiful condition." Standing in front of the unfinished rotunda entrance to the new Delaware Public Archives, the $18 million expansion of the 1938 Leon deValinger Jr. Hall of Records in Dover, McCabe notes the Duke of York transferred his holdings five months later to William Penn to satisfy a debt the crown owed his father. "He was an admiral in the Royal Navy and a friend of the king. He'd loaned money to the king to help finance military activities." The Charter Document, the deed from the Duke of York to William Penn and two 10,000-year leases, also dated 1682, descended through the Penn family in America. The lease for the 'South Tract' or lower Delaware exacts a curious fee: "…paying therefore yearely and every yeare to his said Royall Highness his heires and Assignes one Rose at the feast of St. Michael the Archangell yearely if demanded…" "Hopefully, those are renewable leases," McCabe muses. "As for the rose, I'm guessing it's never been demanded."

In 1811, John Penn, William Penn's great-grandson, turned over the four documents to his attorney, John R. Coates, to recover "some of the Penn Family Fortune from the States of Delaware and Pennsylvania." Sarah Wistar Miller of Media, Pennsylvania, niece of Coates' son-in-law, refused $50,000 for the documents and in 1909 presented them to Delaware Governor S.S. Pennewill. The documents, which constitute the basis of all Delaware's land claims and real estate titles, are on permanent display in the Hall of Records in Dover. "They are the state's chain of title and they belong to all citizens of Delaware," McCabe says. "The Charter is our crown jewel, from the king himself."

Grounded in history, the State House on The Green in Dover (preceding pages) held its inaugural legislative session in May, 1792, providing the General Assembly with its first permanent home since legislators vacated New Castle in 1777. Both a statehouse and a court-house, the Georgian building boasts the expensive architectural embellishment of a two-story, half-octagonal judges' bay on the rear wall. Originally designed by Alexander Givan as the Kent County Court House, the structure took five years to construct and was in continuous use as the state capitol until 1933 when lawmakers moved to their present quarters at Legislative Hall. One of eight state-owned museums today, the State House was restored in 1976 as a bicentennial project. "The building is extremely important to Delaware because it is the site of legislation impacting the lives of men, women and children from different socioeconomic levels and cultural backgrounds," says Madeline Dunn, Delaware State Museums' curator of education.

"Being a part of Delaware politics is extremely rewarding because you can make a difference," says four-term state representative Nancy H. Wagner (left) of Dover. "Because we're so small, we have to work together and no matter whom you talk to, everyone knows everyone." Grand-daughter of a North Carolina legislator, Wagner was weaned on politics. After waging an unsuc-cessful first bid for the state House of Representa-tives' 31st District, the Republican prevailed in 1992. "I really know my constituents and actually walked to every door and asked for their vote," she recalls. "But the minute the election is over, it's over and you work as closely with Democrats as Republicans." In Legislative Hall on the eve of the General Assembly's summer recess, Wagner, now Judiciary Committee chairman, signs for Senate legislation from House clerk Donna Snell before walking the bill to committee members. "People in Delaware are very connected to their elected officials. That's very different from any other state and helps us solve problems in different ways."

Frequent flier, a C-17 Globemaster III prepares to touch down at Dover Air Force Base (preceding pages), a daily destination for the newest cargo and troop transport aircraft in the U.S. Air Force's Air Mobility Command. Assigned to Charleston Air Force Base's 437th Airlift Wing, the 174-foot-long workhorse is capable of rapid, strategic delivery to main installations or front line bases globally and can reverse direction on short, narrow runways.

"She's a very warm person which surprised me. Her putting a human face on the tragedy in Yugoslavia meant a lot to the troops," Dominick A. Pulieri recalls of Hillary Rodham Clinton's visit to Dover Air Force Base (right). One of dozens of welcoming civilians, the president and owner of Grotto Pizza is a member of the base's Honorary Commanders Program that builds ties between the Department of Defense's largest aerial port and community leaders. "To be recognized by the First Lady for their efforts in moving humanitarian relief to the Kosovo refugees was truly special," adds base spokesman Technical Sergeant Don Perrien. Responsible for 25 percent of the nation's strategic airlift capability, Dover Air Force Base covers 3,900 acres in Delaware's capital and moves an average of 18 million tons of cargo monthly.

Mighty wings, the C-5 Galaxy (following pages) is one of the largest aircraft in the world, capable of transporting Army combat equipment anywhere in the world at 518 miles per hour. Three dozen of the 247-foot-long behemoths are assigned to Dover Air Force Base, the only all C-5 wing in the U.S. Air Force. Operational in 1970, the Galaxy can be loaded and off-loaded simultaneously from nose and aft cargo openings and can take off and land in relatively short distances. The giant aircraft saw duty in Operation Desert Shield and Operation Desert Storm in the Persian Gulf and most recently in Yugoslavia. With aerial refueling, only crew endurance limits the length of the aircraft's journey.

Downloading horsepower, NASCAR descends on Dover Downs International Speedway for Winston Cup racing in June and September. "People really get hooked on it," says Kent County sportswriter and author Gene Bryson. "It's fast, it's loud, the cars are colorful and it has a huge impact on the Dover area." The Delaware native has covered the sport for 20 years and recently wrote **_Dover Downs NASCAR_**, a history of the mile-long track that opened in 1969. "Dover's a town of 30,000 and twice a year it grows to four or five times that," he says. "Hotel chains and restaurants race to open new accommodations before a race weekend which generates about $40 million and brings 125,000 people into the area."

In the garage, NASCAR big wheels Jeff Gordon and Dale Jarrett (above) chat over carburetors. "They're friendly rivals. They're also the top two performers in the sport," Bryson says. "Both are class people and conduct themselves in that way. They have a lot of respect for each other." More corporate than ever, NASCAR racing is fueled by big money. "Corporate sponsorship drives the sport," Bryson says. "Huge companies spend about $10 million a year to put their names on cars. Look at the drivers. They're covered with sponsors' names too. It's all about money now."

NASCAR Winston Cup fans gear up for action at Dover Downs, auto racing's Monster Mile. "I love it," says Deanna Leatherman (right), leading the charge from the north Dover facility's campground to the 122,000-seat stadium. "We camp, cook-out and watch our favorite drivers," adds the Bobby Labonte fan from Telford, Pennsylvania. "It's so different from watching it on television. We leave our kids and troubles at home and go down to Dover for a long weekend. It's a bonding experience."

Four-year-old Casey Weatherstein (above) of Baltimore, Maryland also finds the speedway, host to Indy Racing League and Busch Grand National races as well, a fun destination. She signals her favorite driver: Dale Earnhardt in car number three. "Our campground area can accommodate 12,000 to 15,000 people. The number of vehicles is in the thousands," says Dover Downs spokesman Al Robinson. "Our Winston Cup event is always sold out. The appeal is the quality of our seating. We're big enough to be classed as a superspeedway, but small enough to see the whole race from any reserved seat."

NASCAR rivals Jeff Gordon and Dale Jarrett (following pages) test their mettle against Dover Downs' Monster Mile. Tight turns, high banks and a fast track buckle the concrete oval in the driver's seat as one of motorsport's top challenges. The first superspeedway to ditch asphalt, Dover Downs resurfaced its track for $2 million before the 1995 season. High-profile drivers like Gordon, dubbed the "hottest race car driver on the planet" and sponsored by Delaware's Du Pont Company, make their only mid-Atlantic appearances at Dover Downs.

Veteran racing fan Jeff Butcher (right) of York, Pennsylvania cheers Winston Cup driver Bill Elliott as he shifts into second place during the MBNA Platinum 400 at Dover Downs. "He's been my man for the last 10 years – ever since Allan Kulwicki died in a helicopter crash." Butcher met Elliott at a recent NASCAR promotion in York. "Got him to sign a few things for me which increased their value by about 900 percent." He's a regular at the Dover speedway. "No matter where you sit, you can see the whole track. The fans are really cool and the racing's always good."

The racing's also good at human-powered events like the Delaware State Track Championship at Polytech High School near Woodside (following pages). Tracks of a different stripe attract the state's best secondary school athletes who start their engines 13 abreast for the 800-meter race.

"We were on fire," Caesar Rodney High School coach John Coveleski recalls after his Riders routed Tatnall School 11-5 for the 1999 state title (pages 134-135). "It was a toss-up going into the game. Tatnall had more skill but we had a physical edge. Next year, there could be a rematch." Already a powerhouse, the Camden secondary school has won the State Boys Lacrosse Championship three out of the past four years. "Our program is only six years old," says Coveleski, a veteran coach recruited from Delaware State University. "Lacrosse is the fastest growing sport in Delaware and our community chemistry is perfect for success. You need bright but hardened players with a passion for the game. We have a lot of bright, bright kids playing."

"I decided not to be mean and let her go ahead and spray me," Romanita Marshall of Milford (preceding pages) says of her cousin Danita LeGrand's prank. "I was washing my aunt's truck and she came out and started washing the hood. She got the hose and we started playing. It was cool. I was enjoying time with her."

Leaping off the Love Boat, Kimmie Burrows, cousin Faron Marshall and friends Asia Surguy, Katie Sipple, William Sipple and Jason Luff (right) plunge into the Leipsic River behind Sambo's, Kent County's landmark tavern and crab house lauded nationally for its jumbo lump crabcakes. "We try to give the best quality for the best price. We cook the old-fashioned way, over an open flame," says Elva Burrows, Sambo's owner with husband Isaac J. Burrows whose father, Samuel C. "Sambo" Burrows Sr., opened the Leipsic tavern and eatery in 1953. Isaac and Elva took over in 1985. "We're open April 1 through mid-November," Elva says. "And we're packed day and night."

Theodore E. Gregory III of Newark cools off at Killens Pond Water Park near Felton (following pages) where Delaware's only state park with swimming pools lures three thousand people on a hot day. For Gregory, nephew of Wilmington city councilman Theopalis K. Gregory, and his family, the water park is the coolest hot spot around. "We can only handle 1,200 at a time, so we end up turning people away because we're so crowded," park manager Jim Charney says. "When we designed the water park, which opened in 1997, we tried to make sure every age group had an area to utilize." Anchored by Killens Pond, a 66-acre 18th century millpond, the park also offers year-round boating, fishing and camping. "We're different," says Charney. "We're not going to compete with Cape Henlopen State Park and Delaware Seashore State Park because they have the beach, but for an inland park, we're very popular."

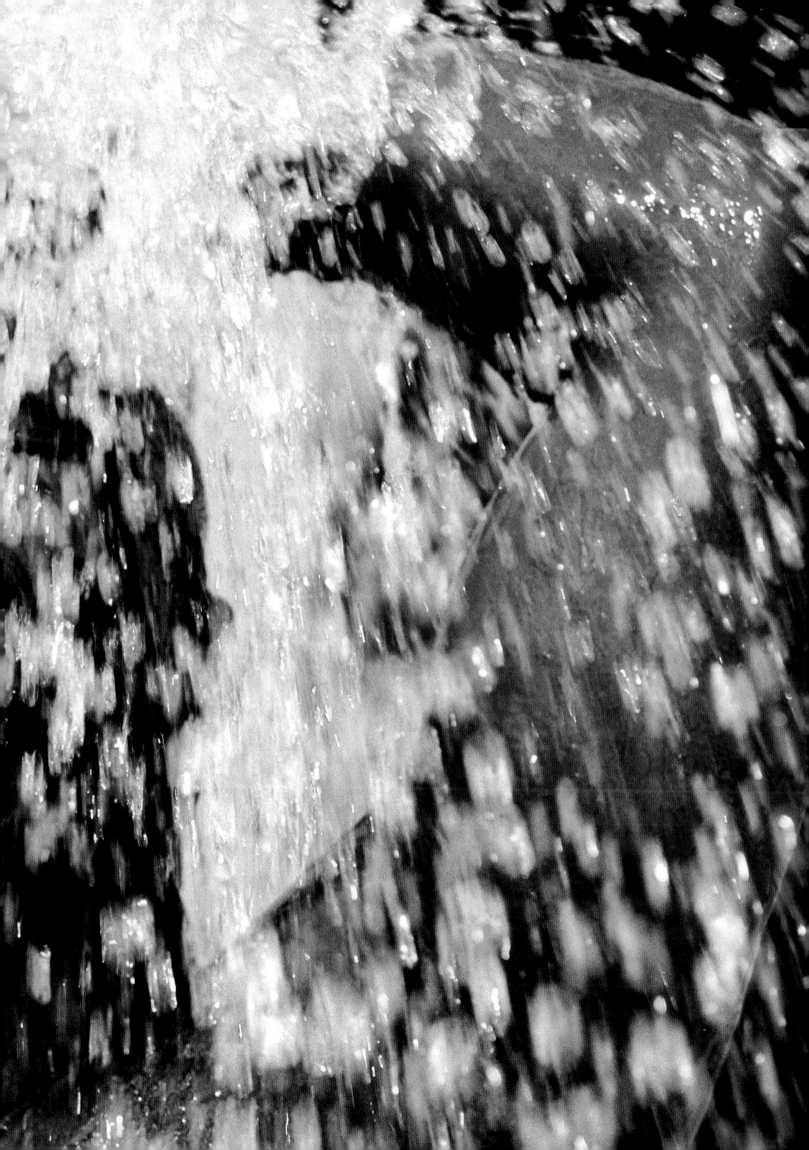

Lake Forest High School senior Neil Gerardi shares a special moment with Rachel Messick (right) at the Junior-Senior Prom. "It's the last chance to get together with classmates before graduation and before everyone goes their separate ways," he says of the school's 30-year tradition. "My juniors work for six months to put this on for the seniors," says Lake Forest art teacher and junior class advisor Lorrie McCartney. "It's the last real fun, let-it-all-hang-out activity before graduation and everyone loves to get dressed up." Gerardi agrees. "It starts out formal but usually about halfway through, people wind up in tank tops and undershirts."

A bevy of beauties (preceding pages) cheers for Lake Forest's newly crowned Prom King and Queen. The coronation highlights an evening that includes an introductory Grand March, dinner and dancing.

"We wanted to create the best party ever in Dover," Frank Fantini (preceding pages) says of the Friends of the Capitol Theater's May benefit to preserve the 1904 Dover Opera House. "We're a theater so we can be theatrical. Each year we will re-create a classic movie. We started with 'The Great Gatsby' and re-created the 1920s on the shore of Silver Lake." As president of the Friends, Fantini leads the $6 million effort to expand and modernize the State Street landmark. Wilmington entrepreneur John W. Rollins Sr. and his wife, Michele, played major supporting roles in that effort with their recent $1 million donation. "When we're finished, in the spring of 2001, it will be a sister theater to the Grand Opera House in Wilmington and will bring a new level of arts to Kent County. Our complex will be the Schwartz Center for the Performing Arts in honor of the family who operated the building as the Capital Theater from 1923 until it closed in 1982."

Betty L. Warren (right) partied with husband Melville and 350 others at the tented event. "We like to go to parties and we like the idea of sponsoring the arts," says Warren. " We're both educators and read about this era. It was great fun." "Dover has two large, successful black-tie fundraisers," adds Fantini, smooching significant other Helen Downing. "There's room in this town for one more major event so we figured it might as well be us. We want to make a statement that everything the Capitol Theater does is first class. Next year, our movie is 'Gone With the Wind.' It's going to be a heck of a party."

Achievement in the air, Delaware State University graduates celebrate in Alumni Stadium after more than 500 received degrees at Delaware's historically black university. "You are each bound by a responsibility to be an agent of change," prominent civil rights attorney and keynote speaker Johnnie L. Cochran told the students. Founded by the 58th General Assembly in 1891 as the "State College for Colored Students," the university has evolved into a fully-integrated, 400-acre campus north of Dover and culls a diverse student population from a dozen states and nine countries.

 Deja McCoy hugs her friend Cashana Lewis (following pages) at the Dover African Festival. The Dover High School sophomore is lead dancer for Sankofa African Drummers and Dancers and wears a *galae* or head wrap of two fabrics to match and accent her ceremonial dress.

 "I noticed a lack of artistic endeavor for minorities so I started the festival in 1991 to create a sense of cultural identity for African-Americans in central Delaware," recalls Dover city councilman Reuben Salters, who visits Africa annually. "I actually started it for the kids with the hope they would get enthused about their culture." They did. Sankofa, formed in 1995, is a major festival attraction. The group of 30 local youngsters, ages eight to 16, also performs statewide. Headliners like the 30-piece Harlem Festival Orchestra and the Trinidad and Tobago Steel Orchestra recently played the Dover event. "Our festival is always the fourth Saturday in June on Legislative Mall and it's always very well received," Salters says. "A lot of people plan their family reunions around it. We draw vendors from Chicago, Detroit, New York and Atlanta."

Farmland covers a lot of ground in Kent County (preceding pages) where more than half of the total acreage is agrarian, the highest percentage in any of Delaware's three counties. Farmers reap the benefits of favorable soil, a long growing season, availability of water and proximity to major metropolitan markets. With 168,000 acres under cultivation in Kent, bumper crops are soybeans, field corn, wheat and barley. Kent County also ranks 42nd nationally in vegetable production.

Camden-Wyoming Little League rookie Robbie Scott (right) takes a night off with fan Dylan Diaz to watch his buddies play ball at the six-diamond complex. On his Sharp Energy team, Robbie suits up for second or third base. "When the team's way ahead, he plays first base," mom Gloria confides. "Little League's an opportunity for kids to get out and play a great sport and meet other kids. It's fun for us as coaches to see them progress," says Camden-Wyoming Little League alumnus Duane Shuba, now a minor league manager and board member of the organization that is a hit with 800 youngsters.

"There are no ghosts here, darn it," laments Jean Gruwell of Wheel of Fortune Farm (following pages), part of a William Penn land grant conveyed to John Chance in 1738. Gruwell and her husband, Hudson, a retired produce broker, bought the 250-acre farm near Leipsic in 1962. Punch and gouge molding and dog-eared door and window framing detail the circa 1750 Georgian manor house. Ax marks score the kitchen's original hand-hewn hemlock beams and brick milk and meat dependencies are still intact on the property bordering tidal Muddy Branch. The lone elm remains from a stand transported by ox cart in 1849 for planting on The Green in Dover. "The best part of living here," Gruwell says, "is the peace and quiet and the view. It's just gorgeous. We're blessed."

Stepping into the past, Mary B. Wagner enters Dover's State House, one of the country's oldest capitols.

Portfolio Books

Post Office Box 156 • Rehoboth Beach, Delaware 19971

film processing by K.R.R.B., Newark, Delaware • color scans by Baltimore Color Plate, Towson, Maryland
proofreading by Ken Mammarella and J.L. Miller • production assistance by Jenna Kelley

printed and bound in Hong Kong by Dai Nippon Printing Co., Ltd.